Trump vs. Obama

In Their Own Words

By Lincoln Roberts

Table of Contents

Quotes on Abortion (Obama)

i. "I think that most Americans recognize that this is a profoundly difficult issue for the women and families who make these decisions. They don't make them casually. And I trust women to make these decisions in conjunction with their doctors and their families and their clergy."
Primary debate, MSNBC, 4/26/2007

ii. "No one is pro-abortion. I think it's always a tragic situation"
Presidential Debate, 10/15/2008

iii. "We should do everything we can to reduce unintended pregnancies and support women who choose to have a child."
Interview with The Catholic Digest, October 2008

iv. "If we can create a situation where young women and young men are acting responsibly and recognize the sacredness of human sexuality, then we can drastically cut the number of abortions.
Interview with The Catholic Digest, October 2008

v. "I do not suggest that the debate surrounding abortion can or should go away, because, no matter how much we may want to fudge it — indeed, while we know that the views of most Americans on the subject are complex and even contradictory — the fact is that, at some level, the views of the two camps are irreconcilable."
Remarks at Notre Dame Commencement, 5/17/2009

vi. "Each side will continue to make its case to the public with passion and conviction, but surely we can do so without reducing those with differing views to caricature."
Remarks at Notre Dame Commencement, 5/17/2009

vii. "Maybe we won't agree on abortion, but we can still agree that this heart-wrenching decision for any woman is not made casually, it has both moral and spiritual dimensions."
Remarks at Notre Dame Commencement, 5/17/2009

Quotes On Abortion (Trump)

i. "One thing about me, I'm a very honorable guy. I'm pro-life, but I changed my view a number of years ago. One of the primary reasons I changed [was] a friend of mine's wife was pregnant, and he didn't really want the baby. He was crying as he was telling me the story. He ends up having the baby and the baby is the apple of his eye. It's the greatest thing that's ever happened to him. And you know here's a baby that wasn't going to be let into life. And I heard this, and some other stories, and I am pro-life."
Christian Broadcasting Network, 4/8/2011

ii. "There are certain things that I don't think can ever be negotiated. Let me put it this way: I am pro life, and pro-life people will find out that I will be very loyal to them, just as I am loyal to other people. I would be appointing judges that feel the way I feel"
Interview with the NY Times, 5/2/2011

iii. "A ban on elective abortions after 20 weeks will protect unborn children. We should not be one of seven countries that allows elective abortions after 20 weeks. It goes against our core values."
Christian Broadcasting Network, July 2015

iv. "Planned Parenthood has to stop with the abortions. A lot of people consider it an abortion clinic."
Meet The Press, August 2015

v. "The answer is that there has to be some form of punishment...for the woman"
Town Hall Meeting, 3/30/2016.
(Editor's note: In fairness, he was answering a question from Chris Matthews who was pressuring him for an answer. Later that day he Tweeted "The woman is a victim in this case as is the life in her womb." The campaign later clarified that doctors, not women, must be punished if Roe v Wade is overturned)

vi. "All children — born and unborn — are made in the holy image of God"
State of the Union Address, 2/5/2019

vii. "As most people know, and for those who would like to know, I am strongly Pro-Life, with the three exceptions – Rape, Incest and protecting the Life of the mother – the same position taken by Ronald Reagan."
Twitter, 5/18/2019

Chapter 2

Business Quotes

Quotes On Business (Trump)

i. I don't do it for the money. I've got enough, much more than I'll ever need. I do it to do it. Deals are my art form. Other people paint beautifully on canvas or write wonderful poetry. I like making deals, preferably big deals. That's how I get my kicks."
The Art Of The Deal, p.1,1987

ii. People think I'm a gambler. I've never gambled in my life. To me, a gambler is someone who plays slot machines. I prefer to own slot machines. It's a very good business being the house.
The Art Of The Deal, p.48, 1987

iii. "The point is you can't be too greedy"
The Art Of The Deal, p.48, 1987

iv. "Money was never a big motivation for me, except as a way to keep score. The real excitement is playing the game."
The Art Of The Deal, p.63, 1987

v. "It's very possible that I could be the first presidential candidate to run and make money on it."
Fortune Magazine, 4/3/2000

vi. "I don't like firing people. It's not a pleasant thing and it's sad. ... In some cases, it's a terrible, terrible situation for the person who gets fired, how strongly they take it. So it's not something that any rational or sane person can love doing, but it also happens to be a fact of life in business."
Boston Herald, 1/7/2004

vii. "There's a beauty in those two words ('You're Fired'). When you utter those words, there's very little that can be said. There's a succinctness to those words"
San Francisco Chronicle, 3/28/2004

viii. "Get going. Move forward. Aim high. Plan for a takeoff. Don't just sit on the runway and hope someone will come along and push the airplane. It simply won't happen. Change your attitude and gain some altitude. Believe me, you'll love it up here."
How To Get Rich, 2004

ix. "I called myself the king of debt. I'm the king of debt. I'm great with debt, nobody knows debt better than me. I made a fortune by using debt. And if things don't work out I renegotiate the debt, I mean that's a smart thing not a stupid thing. And I made a fortune."
CBS This Morning, 6/22/2016

x. "No debts. I have very little debt to anybody. I don't need debt. You know, it's very interesting, I'm so liquid, I don't need debt. And if I need debt, if I want debt, I can get it from banks in New York City very easily."
ABC News, 7/30/2016

xi. "The economic numbers just came out; they're very, very good. Our country is doing unbelievably well, economically. Most of you don't report that, because it doesn't sound good from your perspective. But the country is doing really, really well. We have a lot of very exciting things going on. A lot of companies will be announcing shortly they're moving back into the United States. They're all coming back. They want to be where the action is."
Remarks to reporters, 4/5/2019

Quotes On Business (Obama)

i. "I will eliminate capital-gains taxes for the small businesses and the startups that will create the high-wage, high-tech jobs of tomorrow"
Yes We Can, *p.73, 2008*

ii. "Ninety-eight percent of all American companies have fewer than 100 employees. Over half of all Americans work for a small business. Small businesses are the backbone of our nation's economy and we must protect this great resource.....Helping American small business is part of our movement for change and the end of politics as usual."
Campaign statement referencing Small Business League's support of candidate Obama, 2/26/2008

iii. "It's not that I want to punish your success. I want to make sure that everybody who is behind you, that they've got a chance for success, too. My attitude is that if the economy's good for folks from the bottom up, it's gonna be good for everybody. I think when you spread the wealth around, it's good for everybody."
In conversation caught on camera with "Plumber Joe" Wurzelbach, 10/14/2008

iv. "It's here that companies like Solyndra are leading the way toward a brighter and more prosperous future."
Speech at Solyndra's Headquarters, May, 2010.
(Editor's note: Solyndra later went belly-up)

v. "So I'm not proposing anything radical. I just believe that anybody making over $250,000 a year should go back to the income tax rates we were paying under Bill Clinton. Back when our economy created nearly 23 million new jobs, the biggest budget surplus in history, and plenty of millionaires to boot. ... At the same time, most people agree that we should not raise taxes on middle-class families or small businesses -- not when so many folks are just trying to get by."
White House News Conference, 7/9/2012

vi. "If you were successful, somebody…gave you some help… Somebody invested in roads and bridges. If you've got a business – you didn't build that."
Election campaign speech, 7/13/2012. (Editor's note- "that" refers to the   roads and bridges. This quote is often quoted out of context)

vii.	"The Internet didn't get invented on its own. Government research created
the Internet so that all the companies could make money off the Internet.
The point is, is that when we succeed, we succeed because of our
individual initiative, but also because we do things together."
Election campaign speech, 7/13/2012

viii.	"I think what grows the economy is when you get that tax credit that we put
in place for your kids going to college. I think that grows the economy. I
think what grows the economy is when we make sure small businesses are
getting a tax credit for hiring veterans who fought for our country. That
grows our economy."
Presidential Debate, 10/17/2012

ix.	"We should raise the minimum wage so that no one who works full-time
has to live in poverty."
Weekly radio address, 7/19/2014

x.	"We could have done nothing, which some people said we should do, and
let those (auto) companies fail, but think about what that would have
meant for this country -- the suppliers, the distributors, the communities
that depend on the workers who patronize the restaurants and shop at the
stores. All those companies would have gone under also…"
Remarks at Ford auto plant, 1/7/2015

xi.	"Here's a guy (Trump) who says he's a great businessman. But it seems
like a lot of his business is built around stiffing small businesses and
workers out of what he owes them -- work they've done. He thinks it's
cute, or smart, or funny to basically not pay somebody who's done work
for him and say, go ahead and sue me because I got more money than
you, and you can't do anything about it. It's not fair."
Rally in support of Hillary Clinton, 11/3/2016

Chapter 3

Children, Parents & Family Quotes

Quotes on Children, Parents & Family (Obama)

i. "In my daughters I see her every day, her joy, her capacity for wonder. I won't try to describe how deeply I mourn her passing still. I know that she was the kindest, most generous spirit I have ever known, and that what is best in me I owe to her."
About his mother--Preface to <u>Dreams Of My Father</u>, 2004 edition

ii. "It doesn't make sense to not give them information. You still want to teach them the morals and the values to make good decisions…(but) include other, you know, information about contraception because, look, I've got two daughters -- 9 years old and 6 years old. I'm going to teach them first of all about values and morals, but if they make a mistake, I don't want them punished with a baby. I don't want them punished with an STD at the age of 16."
CNN, discussing sex education at a town hall, 3/29/2008

iii. "It's up to us to say to our daughters, don't ever let images on TV tell you what you are worth, because I expect you to dream without limit and reach for those goals."
Father's Day speech, Apostolic Church of God, Chicago, 6/15/2008

iv. "It's up to us to tell our sons, those songs on the radio may glorify violence, but in my house we give glory to achievement, self-respect and hard work. It's up to us to set these high expectations. And that means meeting those expectations ourselves. That means setting examples of excellence in our own lives."
Father's Day speech, Apostolic Church of God, Chicago, 6/15/2008

v. "We need to show our kids that you're not strong by putting other people down — you're strong by lifting them up. That's our responsibility as fathers."
Father's Day speech, Apostolic Church of God, Chicago, 6/15/2008

vi. "As fathers, we need to be involved in our children's lives not just when it's convenient or easy, and not just when they're doing well — but when it's difficult and thankless, and they're struggling. That is when they need us most."
Parade Magazine, 2009

vii.   "Above all, children need our unconditional love — whether they succeed
        or make mistakes; when life is easy and when life is tough."
        Father's Day address, 2011

viii.   "We've been married now twenty years, and like every marriage you have
        your ups and you have your downs, but if you work through the tough
        times, the respect and love that you feel deepens."
        Interview with Barbara Walters, 2012

ix.   "Our journey is not complete until our wives, our mothers and daughters
        can earn a living equal to their efforts. Our journey is not complete until
        our gay brothers and sisters are treated like anyone else under the law - for
        if we are truly created equal, then surely the love we commit to one another
        must be equal as well."
        2nd Inaugural Address, 1/20/13

x.   "I'm still practicing, I'm still learning, still getting corrected in terms of
        how to be a fine husband and a good father. But I will tell you this:
        Everything else is unfulfilled if we fail at family, if we fail at that
        responsibility."
        Morehouse College Commencement Speech, 5/19/2013

xi.   …what I did learn was that unconditional love makes up for an awful lot,
        and I got that from her.
        About his mother. CNN Interview, 12/26/2016

Quotes on Children, Parents & Family (Trump)

i. "My mother had a sense of the grand. I can remember her watching the coronation of Queen Elizabeth and being so fascinated by it. My father had no interest in that kind of thing at all."
The Art Of The Deal, p.80, 1987

ii. "I was never intimidated by my father, the way most people were…I stood up to him and he respected that."
The Art Of The Deal, p.71, 1987

iii. "There is nothing to compare with family if they happen to be competent, because you can trust family in a way you can never trust anyone else."
The Art Of The Deal, p.206, 1987

iv. "I'll tell you what I've learned: Children are tough. Much tougher than people think. ... I'm a really good father, but not a really good husband. You've probably figured out my children really like me--love me--a lot."
New York Magazine, 12/3/2004

v. "The hardest thing for me about raising kids has been finding the time. I know friends who leave their business so they can spend more time with their children, and I say, 'Gimme a break!' My children could not love me more if I spent fifteen times more time with them."
New York Magazine, 12/3/2004

vi. "I've said that if Ivanka weren't my daughter, perhaps I'd be dating her."
The View, 3/6/2006

vii. "Marriage is a contract unlike any other contract in life. It's a legally binding contract that knows nothing of love. If the love dies, all you have left is a resentful ex-spouse & the marriage certificate"
Think Big And Kick Ass: In Business And Life pp. 31-32, 2007

viii. "It is okay to let your children know they are special. It is a part of being a loving parent, but do not overdo it. To constantly lavish praise on your children for every little thing they do is too much. Do not be easy on them. Let your children work hard to gain your praise. They will value it more."
Think Big And Kick Ass: In Business And Life, p.66, 2007

ix. "That's why I'm so screwed up, because I had a father that pushed me pretty hard,"
Think Big And Kick Ass: In Business And Life, p.321, 2007

x. "It has not been easy for me; it has not been easy for me. And you know I started off in Brooklyn, my father gave me a small loan of a million dollars."
NH Town Hall Meeting, 10/26/2015

xi. "The happiest people I know are those people who have great families and real values. I've seen it. I know it. People who have a loving spouse and have children they really love are happy people."
Crippled America, How To Make America Great Again, p.128, 11/3/2015

xii. "I want to start by, as always, thanking my family. My kids, they're not kids anymore, but they're kids as far as I'm concerned. They'll always be my kids."
Speech after winning Indiana Primary- 5/3/2016

xiii. "I don't want to take children away from their parents (but) when you prosecute the parents for coming in illegally, which should happen, you have to take the children away."
National Federation of Independent Businesses, 6/19/2018

Chapter 4

Climate Change/ Environment Quotes

Quotes on Climate Change and the Environment (Trump)

i.   "The concept of global warming was created by and for the Chinese in order to make U.S. manufacturing non-competitive."
Twitter, 11/6/2012

ii.   "It's freezing outside, where the hell is 'global warming'?"
Twitter, 5/25/2013

iii.   "We should be focused on magnificently clean and healthy air and not distracted by the expensive hoax that is global warming!"
Twitter, 12/6/2013

iv.   "Give me clean, beautiful and healthy air - not the same old climate change …bullshit! I am tired of hearing this nonsense."
Twitter, 1/29/2014

v.   "Obama said in his State of the Union that 'global warming is a fact.' Sure, about as factual as 'if you like your healthcare, you can keep it.'"
Twitter, 1/30/2014

vi.   "I believe in clean air. Immaculate air. But I don't believe in climate change."
CNN Interview, 9/24/2015

Quotes on Climate Change and the Environment (Obama)

i.   "The shift to a cleaner energy economy won't happen overnight, and it
will require tough choices along the way. But the debate is
settled. Climate change is a fact."
State of the Union, 1/28/2014

ii.   "This is not some distant problem of the future. This is a problem that is
affecting Americans right now. Whether it means increased flooding,
greater vulnerability to drought, more severe wildfires- all these things
are having an impact on Americans as we speak."
USA Today, 5/6/2014

iii.   "When Americans are called on to innovate, that's what we do -whether
it's making more fuel-efficient cars or more fuel-efficient appliances, or
making sure that we are putting in place the kinds of equipment that
prevents harm to the ozone layer and eliminates acid rain."
WH Press Conference, 6/2/2014

iv.   "Part of what's unique about climate change, though, is the nature of
some of the opposition to action. It's pretty rare that you'll encounter
somebody who says the problem you're trying to solve simply doesn't
exist. When President Kennedy set us on a course for the moon, there
were a number of people who made a serious case that it wouldn't be
worth it; it was going to be too expensive, it was going to be too hard, it
would take too long. But nobody ignored the science. I don't remember
anybody saying that the moon wasn't there or that it was made of
cheese."
UC Irvine Commencement Address, 6/14/2014

v.   "Today, about 40 percent of America's carbon pollution comes from our
power plants. There are no federal limits to the amount those plants can
pump into the air. None. We limit the amount of toxic chemicals like
mercury, and sulfur, and arsenic in our air and water, but power plants
can dump as much carbon pollution into our atmosphere as they want.
It's not smart, it's not right, it's not safe, and I determined it needs to
stop."
League of Conservation Voters Capital Dinner, 6/25/2014

vi.   "There's one issue that will define the contours of this century more
       dramatically than any other, and that is the urgent and growing threat of
       a changing climate."
       U.N. Climate Change Summit, 9/23/2014

vii.   "No challenge – no challenge – poses a greater threat to future
       generations than climate change. 2014 was the planet's warmest year on
       record. Now, one year doesn't make a trend, but this does – 14 of the 15
       warmest years on record have all fallen in the first 15 years of this
       century."
       State of the Union Address, 1/20/2015

Chapter 5

Constitution Quotes

Quotes On the Constitution (Obama)

i. "I don't think the two views are contradictory, to say that it was a remarkable political document that paved the way for where we are now, and to say that it also reflected the fundamental flaw of this country that continues to this day."
NPR Program, Slavery & The Constitution, September 2001

ii. "As Americans, we can take enormous pride in the fact that courage has been inspired by our own struggle for freedom, by the tradition of democratic law secured by our forefathers and enshrined in our Constitution. It is a tradition that says all men are created equal under the law and that no one is above it."
Senate floor, 2/3/2005

iii. "I was a constitutional law professor, which means unlike the current president I actually respect the Constitution." *Campaign fundraising event, 3/30/2007*

iv. "The president does not have power under the Constitution to unilaterally authorize a military attack in a situation that does not involve stopping an actual or imminent threat to the nation. As commander in chief, the president does have a duty to protect and defend the United States. In instances of self-defense, the president would be within his constitutional authority to act before advising Congress or seeking its consent."
Boston Globe, 12/20/2007

v. "I take the Constitution very seriously. The biggest problems that we're facing right now have to do with (a president) trying to bring more and more power into the executive branch and not go through Congress at all."
Lancaster, PA Town Hall, 3/31/2008

vi. "I think a basic principle of our Constitution is that nobody is above the law"
philly.com, 4/14/2008

vii. "If you look at the victories and failures of the civil rights movement, and its litigation strategy in the court, I think where it succeeded was to vest formal rights in previously dispossessed peoples, so that I would now have the right to vote, I would now be able to sit at a lunch counter and order and as long as I could pay for it I'd be okay… It didn't break free from the essential constraints that were placed by the founding fathers in the Constitution."
Washington Monthly, 10/27/2008

viii. "Generally, the Constitution is a charter of negative liberties, says what the states can't do to you, says what the federal government can't do to you. But it doesn't say what the state or federal government must do on your behalf."
Washington Monthly, 10/27/2008

ix. "If we don't uphold our Constitution and our values, that over time, that will make us less safe and that will be a recruitment tool for organizations like Al Qaeda. That's what I have to keep my eye on."
NBC Today Show, 2/2/2009

x. "Unlike most countries, we're not all of the same race or religion and we don't always come from the same places, as many of us are immigrants. What holds us all together is a belief in certain ideals and certain values, and the constitution really is what sets us apart by saying that every single person is treated with respect, every single individual has certain rights and that the government has to follow certain rules in how it interacts with its citizens."
Interview with two elementary school age students from Scholastic Magazine, 9/17/2011

xi. "The strongest weapon against hateful speech is not repression; it is more speech."
UN General Assembly, 9/25/2012

xii. "I do not accept that we cannot find a common sense way to preserve our traditions, including our basic second amendment freedoms and the rights of law abiding gun owners, while at the same time reducing the gun violence that unleashes so much mayhem on a regular basis."
Washington Navy Yard Massacre- The Aftermath, Huffington Post, 9/23/2013, remarks on 9/22/2013

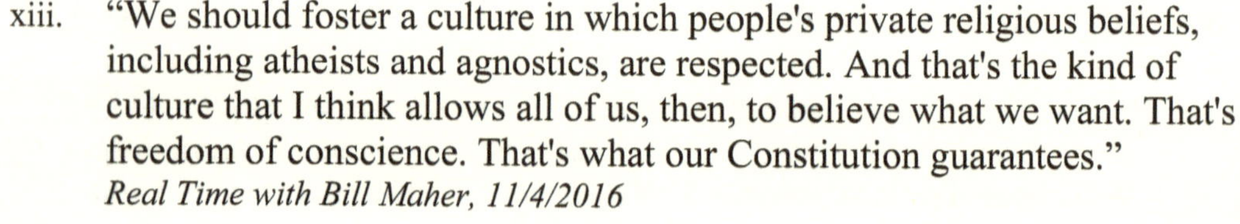

xiii.   "We should foster a culture in which people's private religious beliefs, including atheists and agnostics, are respected. And that's the kind of culture that I think allows all of us, then, to believe what we want. That's freedom of conscience. That's what our Constitution guarantees."
Real Time with Bill Maher, 11/4/2016

Quotes On the Constitution (Trump)

i. "The Second Amendment to our Constitution is clear. The right of the people to keep and bear Arms shall not be infringed upon. Period."
Official Statement Released by Trump Campaign, 9/25/2015

ii. "You know, the Constitution - there's nothing like it. But it doesn't necessarily give us the right to commit suicide as a country, OK? ... We're not gonna allow the people to come into our country. ... And if people want to come in, there's gonna be 'Extreme vetting.'"
Meet The Press w/Chuck Todd, 7/24/2016

iii. "I don't think we should have justices appointed that decide what they want to hear. It's all about the Constitution the way it was meant to be. And those are the people that I will appoint."
Presidential Debate, 9/19/2016

iv. "Nobody should be allowed to burn the American flag - if they do, there must be consequences - perhaps loss of citizenship or year in jail!"
Twitter, 11/29/2016

v. "I am proud to announce that I will be very soon signing an executive order requiring colleges and universities to support free speech if they want federal research funds"
Conservative Political Action Conference Speech, 3/2/2019

vi. "I don't think that the mainstream media is free speech because it's so crooked. It's so dishonest."
White House Social Media Summit, 7/11/2019

vii. "To me free speech is not when you see something good and then you purposefully write bad. To me that's very dangerous speech."
White House Social Media Summit, 7/11/2019

viii. "Article 2 allows me to do whatever I want. Article 2 would have allowed me to fire him (Robert Mueller)."
ABC News with George Stephanopoulos, 6/16/2019

Chapter 6

Democracy Quotes

Quotes On Democracy (Trump)

i. "The American Dream is freedom, prosperity, peace — and liberty and justice for all. That's a big dream. It's not always easy to achieve, but that's the ideal. More than any country in history, we've made gains toward a democracy that is enviable throughout the world."
Forbes, 3/22/07

ii. "The electoral college is a disaster for democracy"
Twitter, 11/6/2012

iii. "This election will determine whether we're a free nation or whether we have only the illusion of democracy but are in fact controlled by a small handful of global special interests rigging the system, and our system is rigged. This is reality."
Campaign speech, 10/13/2013

iv. "Hillary Clinton put her emails on a secret server to cover up her pay-for-play scandals in the State Department. Nothing threatens the integrity of our democracy more than when government officials put their public office up for sale."
National Security Speech, 9/7/2016

v. "The criminal conduct of Hillary Clinton threatens the foundations of democracy. I mean that"
Campaign Rally, 10/25/2016

vi. "In addition to winning the Electoral College in a landslide, I won the popular vote if you deduct the millions of people who voted illegally"
Twitter, 11/27/2016

vii. "Erasing national borders does not make people safer or more prosperous. It undermines democracy and trades away prosperity."
Presidential Rally, 2/18/2017

viii. "Every time voter fraud occurs, it cancels out the vote of a lawful citizen and undermines democracy - can't let that happen."
First Meeting of Election Integrity Commission, 7/19/2017

ix.   "I used to like the idea of the Popular Vote, but now realize the Electoral College is far better for the U.S.A."
Twitter, 3/20/2019

Quotes On Democracy (Obama)

i. "In a country as diverse as ours, there will always be passionate arguments about how we draw the line when it comes to government action. That is how our democracy works. But our democracy might work a bit better if we recognized that all of us possess values that are worthy of respect: if liberals at least acknowledged that the recreational hunter feels the same way about his gun as they feel about their library books, and if conservatives recognized that most women feel as protective of their right to reproductive freedom as evangelicals do of their right to worship."
The Audacity Of Hope, p.57, 2006

ii. "I always believe that ultimately, if people are paying attention, then we get good government and good leadership. And when we get lazy, as a democracy and civically start taking shortcuts, then it results in bad government and politics."
MSNBC interview, 9/25/2006

iii. "We have proved that the true strength of our nation comes not from the scale of our wealth but from the power of our ideals - opportunity, democracy, liberty and hope."
Election Victory Speech, 11/4/2008

iv. "The strongest democracies flourish from frequent and lively debate, but they endure when people of every background and belief find a way to set aside smaller differences in service of a greater purpose."
Presidential News Conference, 2/9/2009

v. "Now, I swore an oath to uphold the laws on the books... Now, I know some people want me to bypass Congress and change the laws on my own... Believe me, the idea of doing things on my own is very tempting. I promise you. Not just on immigration reform. But that's not how - that's not how our system works. That's not how our democracy functions. That's not how our Constitution is written."
National Council of La Raza, 7/25/2011

vi. "No party has a monopoly on wisdom. No democracy works without compromise."
Democrat Convention Speech, 9/6/2012

vii.   "Mandela's commitment to democracy was ratified not only by his election, but by his willingness to step down from power."
Transcript of remarks after Mandela's death, 12/10/2013

viii.   "It should be the power of our vote, not the size of our bank accounts, that drives our democracy."
State of the Union Address, 1/28/2014

ix.   "The commitment of the United States to Europe is enduring and it's rooted in the values we share; our commitment to democracy, our commitment to rule of law, our commitment to the dignity of all people in our own countries and around the world."
Obama/Merkel Joint Press Conference, 11/17/2016

x.   "No individual – not Mandela, not Obama – are entirely immune to the corrupting influences of absolute power, if you can do whatever you want and everyone's too afraid to tell you when you're making a mistake. No one is immune from the dangers of that."
Nelson Mandela Annual Lecture, 7/17/2018

Chapter 7

Gun Quotes

Quotes On Guns (Obama)

i.   "I believe in the Second Amendment…How did we get to the place where people think requiring a comprehensive background check means taking away people's guns?"
Transcript of remarks prior to "Executive Action," 1/5/2016

ii.   "We do not have to accept this carnage as the price of freedom."
Transcript of remarks prior to "Executive Action," 1/5/2016

iii.   "Are you suggesting that the notion that we are creating a plot to take everybody's guns away so that we can impose martial law isn't a conspiracy? Yes, that is a conspiracy. I would hope that you would agree."
Town Hall on Gun Control, w/ Chris Cuomo, CNN, 1/8/2016

iv.   "We're not going to eliminate gun violence, but we will lessen it. If we take the number from 30,000 [gun-related deaths per year in the U.S.] down to 28,000, that's 2,000 families who don't have to go through what the families of Newtown [Connecticut] or San Bernardino [California] or Charleston [South Carolina] went through."
Town Hall on Gun Control, w/ Chris Cuomo, CNN, 1/8/2016

v.   "Michelle and I are campaigning out in Iowa . . . At one point Michelle turned to me and said, 'You know, if I was living in a farmhouse where the sheriff's department is pretty far away and somebody could just turn off the highway and come up to the farm, I'd want to have a shotgun or a rifle to make sure I was protected and my family was protected.' And she was absolutely right."
Town Hall on Gun Control, CNN, 1/8/2016

vi.   "I visited Newtown two days after what happened, so it was still very raw. It's the only time I've ever seen Secret Service cry on duty . . . It continues to haunt me. It was one of the worst days of my presidency."
Town Hall on Gun Control, CNN, 1/8/2016

vii.   "Part of my faith and hope in America is not that we achieve a perfect union, but that we get better. And we can do better than we're doing right now, if we come together."
Town Hall on Gun Control, CNN, 1/8/2016

Quotes On Guns (Trump)

i. "Gun and magazine bans are a total failure. ... Opponents of gun rights try to come up with scary sounding phrases like 'assault weapons,' 'military-style weapons' and 'high capacity magazines' to confuse people."
Policy Paper, 9/18/2015

ii. "No matter what you do, guns, [or] no guns, [it] doesn't matter. You have people that are mentally ill and they're going to come through the cracks and they're going to do things that people will not even believe are possible."
Meet the Press interview with Chuck Todd, 9/28/15

iii. "I will get rid of gun-free zones on schools, and — you have to — and on military bases. My first day, it gets signed, OK? My first day. There's no more gun-free zones."
Campaign Rally, 1/7/2016

iv. If (Hillary) gets to pick her judges, nothing you can do, folks, although the Second Amendment people — maybe there is, I don't know.
Campaign Rally, 8/11/2016

v. "I have the endorsement of the NRA which I'm very proud of, these are very, very good people and they're protecting the Second Amendment."
Presidential Debate, 9/26/2016

vi. "And I'm a fan of the NRA. I mean, there's no bigger fan. I'm a big fan of the NRA."
White House meeting transcript, 2/28/2018

vii. "We cannot let those killed in El Paso, Texas, and Dayton, Ohio, die in vain…Republicans and Democrats must come together and get strong background checks, perhaps marrying this legislation with desperately needed immigration reform. We must have something good, if not GREAT, come out of these two tragic events!"
Twitter, 8/5/2019

viii. "It's the people that pull the trigger, not the gun that pulls the trigger so we have a very, very big mental health problem and Congress is working on various things and I will be looking at it"
Remarks prior to taking helicopter, 8/18/2019

Chapter 8

Healthcare Quotes

Quotes On Healthcare (Trump)

i. "If you can't take care of your sick in the country, forget it, it's all over. I mean, it's no good. So I'm very liberal when it comes to health care. I believe in universal health care. I believe in whatever it takes to make people well and better."
Larry King Show, 10/8/1999

ii. "We must have universal healthcare…I'm a conservative on most issues but a liberal on this one. We should not hear so many stories of families ruined by healthcare expenses…"
The America We Deserve, 2000

iii. "In order to save Medicare and stop record premium increases--we must repeal ObamaCare."
Twitter, 10/6/2011

iv. "Wow, the Supreme Court passed Obama Care. I guess Justice Roberts wanted to be a part of Georgetown society more than anyone knew."
Twitter, 6/28/2012

v. "A friend of mine was in Scotland recently. He got very, very sick. They took him by ambulance and he was there for four days. He was really in trouble and they released him and he said, 'Where do I pay?' And they said, 'There's no charge.' Not only that, he said it was like great doctors, great care. I mean we could have a great system in this country."
Letterman, 1/8/2015

vi. "What I'd like to see is a private system without the artificial lines around every state."
First Republican Primary Debate, 8/6/2015

vii.   "The government's gonna pay for it. But we're going to save so much money on the other side. But for the most it's going to be a private plan and people are going to be able to go out and negotiate great plans with lots of different competition with lots of competitors with great companies and they can have their doctors, they can have plans, they can have everything."
60 Minutes interview with Scott Pelley, 9/27/2015

viii.   "We're going to have great plans. They're going to be much less expensive and they're going to be much better because the Obama plan is unaffordable and it's a disaster… But there will be a group of people that is not doing well, that has no money…We cannot let them die in the streets. And we'll work out either through Medicare, which we'll save or something… And I say to the Republicans all the time. And by the way I get standing ovations from Republicans, from Republican groups. I got one yesterday. I said we can't let people die in the streets… We're going to take care of them. We're going to take care of them. We have to take care of them. Now, that's not single payer. That's not anything. That's just human decency. And I'll tell you what. Every single time I say that, I say to people in the audience -- I say, 'So what do you think?' They all stand up and give me a standing ovation, OK?"
MSNBC town hall with Joe Scarborough & Mika Brzezinski, 2/17/2016

ix.   "Obamacare is a disaster. You know it, we all know it. It's going up at numbers that nobody's ever seen, worldwide. It's -- nobody has ever seen numbers like this for health care. It's only getting worse… We have to repeal it and replace it with something absolutely much less expensive. And something that works, where your plan can actually be tailored. We have to get rid of the lines around the state, artificial lines, where we stop insurance companies from coming in and competing."
Second Presidential Debate, 10/9/2016

x.   "President Obama said you keep your doctor, keep your plan. The whole thing was a fraud and it doesn't work."
Second Presidential Debate, 10/9/2016

xi.   "We're not going to have, like, a two-day period and we're not going to have a two-year period where there's nothing. It will be repealed and replaced. And we'll know. And it'll be great health care for much less money. So it'll be better health care, much better, for less money. Not a bad combination."
60 Minutes interview with Leslie Stahl, 11/13/2016

xii.   "It's an unbelievably complex subject. Nobody knew that health care could be so complicated."
Meeting with governors at White House, 2/28/2017

xiii.   As I have always said, let ObamaCare fail and then come together and do a great healthcare plan. Stay tuned!
Twitter, 7/18/2017

Quotes On Healthcare (Obama)

i. "No matter how we reform health care, I intend to keep this promise: If you like your doctor, you'll be able to keep your doctor; if you like your health care plan, you'll be able to keep your health care plan."
Town hall in Green Bay, 6/11/2009

ii. "Michelle and I don't want anyone telling us who our family's doctor should be – and no one should decide that for you either. Under our proposals, if you like your doctor, you keep your doctor. If you like your current insurance, you keep that insurance. Period, end of story."
Weekly Presidential Address, 7/18/2009

iii. "Medicare and Social Security faced the same kind of criticism. Before Medicare came into law, one Republican warned that 'one of these days, you and I are going to spend our sunset years telling our children and our children's children what it once was like in America when men were free.' That was Ronald Reagan. And eventually, Ronald Reagan came around to Medicare and thought it was pretty good, and actually helped make it better. So that's what's going to happen with the Affordable Care Act. And once it's working really well, I guarantee you they will not call it Obamacare."
Remarks at Prince George Community College, 9/26/2013

iv. "I am sorry that they are finding themselves in this situation based on assurances they got from me…We've got to work hard to make sure that they know we hear them and that we're going to do everything we can to deal with folks who find themselves in a tough position as a consequence of this."
Interview with Chuck Todd, 11/7/2013

v. "Now, some people may say, well, I've seen my copays go up, or my networks have changed. But these are decisions that are made by your employers. It's not because of Obamacare. They're not determined by the Affordable Care Act."
Remarks on the Affordable Care Act, Miami Dade College, 10/20/2016
(Editor's note: As a result of Obamacare, approximately 4 million people lost their plans because their insurance companies chose to discontinue plans that did not comply with the ACA's requirements or raised the cost so high that employers chose to purchase lower cost plans. This meant that perhaps as many as 3% of those already insured could now only "keep their doctor" if they chose not to use their employer's new inferior plan and found a more expensive plan on their own, or paid out of pocket. As of 2018, approximately 20 million people who were not insured are now insured.)

vi. "We're not going to go back to discriminating against Americans with preexisting conditions. We're not going to go back to a time when people's coverage was dropped when they got sick. We're not going to go back to a situation where we're reinstating lifetime limits in the fine print so that you think you have insurance, and then you get really sick or you kid gets really sick, and you hit the limit that the insurance company set, and next thing you know they're not covering you anymore, and you got to figure out how you come up with another $100,000 or $200,000 to make sure that your child lives. We're not going to go back to that."
Remarks on the Affordable Care Act, Miami Dade College, 10/20/2016

vii. "I have always said that for all the good the Affordable Care Act is doing right now, for as big of a step forward as it was, it's still just a first step...It's like buying a starter home. It's a lot better than not having a home. But over time, you hope you can make some improvements."
Remarks on the Affordable Care Act, Miami Dade College, 10/20/2016

viii. "So the challenge of getting it passed was always the fact that unlike other advanced countries, we didn't start with a system in which everybody was covered. And we have a very complicated marketplace and third-party insurers. What that meant was that even after we had gotten the law passed, anything that dissatisfied people about the health care system could be attributed to, quote unquote, 'Obamacare' — even if it had nothing to do with Obamacare."
Vox Interview with Sarah Kliff and Ezra Klein, 1/6/2017

ix. "Well, let's back up and say that there's a reason why, for 100 years, no president could get expansion of health care coverage beyond the work that had been done through Medicare and Medicaid, targeting primarily seniors. And the reason was that this is hard."
Vox Interview with Sarah Kliff and Ezra Klein, 1/6/2017

x. "Thanks to this law, more than ninety percent of Americans are insured – the highest rate in our history. Thanks to this law, the days when women could be charged more than men and Americans with pre-existing conditions could be denied coverage altogether are relics of the past. Seniors have bigger discounts on their prescription drugs. Young people can stay on their parents' plans until they turn 26 years old. And Americans who already had insurance received an upgrade as well – from free preventive care, like mammograms and vaccines, to improvements in the quality of care in hospitals that has averted nearly 100,000 deaths so far."
Remarks on the 7th anniversary of Obamacare, 5/23/2017

Chapter 9

Heroes
Quotes

Quotes On Heroes (Obama)

i. "She was one of those quiet heroes that we have all across America, who -- they're not famous, their names aren't in the newspapers, but each and every day they work hard... They sacrifice for their children and their grandchildren. They aren't seeking the limelight. All they try to do is just do the right thing."
Remarks about his maternal grandmother who raised him, on her passing, the evening before his election, 11/3/08

ii. "Lincoln said to a nation far more divided than ours, 'We are not enemies but friends. ... Though passion may have strained, it must not break our bonds of affection'"
Presidential Victory Speech, 11/4/2008

iii. (On Lincoln) "There is a wisdom there and a humility about his approach to government, even before he was president, that I just find very helpful."
CBS interview with Steve Croft, 11/16/2008

iv. "Heroism is here"
Memorial Service for Victims of Tucson shooting, 1/12/2011

v. "(Mandela) is a personal hero, but I'm not unique in that regard, I think he's a hero for the world and…when he passes, we know his legacy will linger on throughout the ages"
News conference, 6/27/2013

vi. "(Dr. King) started small, rallying others who believed their efforts mattered, pressing on through challenges and doubts to change our world for the better, … a permanent inspiration for the rest of us to keep pushing towards justice."
Twitter, 1/15/2018

Quotes On Heroes (Trump)

i.   "Well, I don't like heroes, I don't like the concept of heroes, the concept of heroes is never great, but certainly you can respect certain people and certainly there are certain people — but I've learnt a lot from my father — my father was a builder in Brooklyn and Queens — he did houses and housing and I learnt a lot about negotiation from my father."
Times of London, 1/16/17

ii.   "[Jackson] was one of our great Presidents…Today, the portrait of this orphan son who rose to the Presidency hangs proudly in the Oval Office, opposite the portrait of another great American, Thomas Jefferson."
Remarks in Oval Office, 3/15/2017

iii.   "(Lincoln) was a man who was of great intelligence, which most presidents would be. But he was a man of great intelligence, but he was also a man that did something that was a very vital thing to do at that time. Ten years before or 20 years before, what he was doing would never have even been thought possible. So he did something that was a very important thing to do, and especially at that time."
Trump Tower interview with Bob Woodward and Robert Costa, 4/4/16

iv.   "Frederick Douglass is an example of somebody who has done an amazing job and is being recognized more and more, I notice"
Remarks on Black History Month, 2/1/2017

v.   "I think Harriet Tubman is fantastic…very very courageous, believe me."
Women's History Month Speech, 3/29/17

vi.   "We are a people whose heroes live not only in the past, but all around us, defending hope, pride, and defending the American way. They work in every trade; they sacrifice to raise a family. They care for our children at home. They defend our flag abroad. They are strong moms and brave kids. They are firefighters and police officer's and border agents, medics, and Marines. Above all else, they are Americans. This capital, the city, this nation, belongs entirely to them."
State of the Union Address, 1/30/2018

Chapter 10

Immigration Quotes

Quotes On Immigration (Trump)

i. "When Mexico sends its people, they're not sending their best… they're bringing drugs. They're bringing crime. They're rapists. And some, I assume, are good people."
Campaign launch announcement, 1/16/2015

ii. "Why do we want people from Haiti here? …We should have more people from places like Norway."
Oval office discussion w/members of Congress, 1/11/2018
(Editors note: The President denied the most controversial part of the quote, which I have therefore removed.)

iii. "Whether it is asylum or anything you want, illegal immigration, we can't take you anymore. Our country is full. Our area is full. The sector is full. We can't take you anymore. Sorry, can't happen. So turn around, that's the way it is."
Remarks on border security, 4/5/2019

iv. "Our plan includes a sweeping modernization of our dysfunctional **legal** immigration process… Under the senseless rules of the current system, we're not able to give preference to a doctor, a researcher, a student who graduated number one in his class from the finest colleges in the world -- anybody."
Modernizing Our Legal Immigration System for A Stronger America, 5/16/2019

v. "Unfortunately, the current immigration rules allow foreign workers to substitute for Americans seeking entry-level jobs… foreign workers are coming in and they're taking the jobs that would normally go to American workers."
Modernizing Our Legal Immigration System for A Stronger America, 5/16/2019

vi. "Priority will also be given to higher-wage workers, ensuring we never undercut American labor. To protect benefits for American citizens, immigrants must be financially self-sufficient."
Modernizing Our Legal Immigration System for A Stronger America, 5/16/2019

Quotes On Immigration (Obama)

i.   "We are a generous and welcoming people here in the US, but those who enter the country illegally, and those who employ them, disrespect the rule of law and they are showing disregard for those who are following the law."
Speech as Senator, 12/15/2005

ii.   "... we simply cannot allow people to pour into the U.S. undetected, undocumented and unchecked. Americans are right to demand better border security and better enforcement of the immigration laws."
Speech as Senator, 12/15/2005

iii.   "Real reform means strong border security, and we can build on the progress my administration has already made -- putting more boots on the Southern border than at any time in our history and reducing illegal crossings to their lowest levels in 40 years,"
State of the Union, 2/12/2013

iv.   "Real reform means establishing a responsible pathway to earned citizenship -- a path that includes passing a background check, paying taxes and a meaningful penalty, learning English, and going to the back of the line behind the folks trying to come here legally…"
State of the Union, 2/12/2013

v.   "To watch those families broken apart in real time puts to us a very simple question: are we a nation that accepts the cruelty of ripping children from their parents' arms, or are we a nation that values families, and works to keep them together? Do we look away, or do we choose to see something of ourselves and our children?"
Twitter, 6/20/2018

vi.   "Our ability to imagine ourselves in the shoes of others, to say 'there but for the grace of God go I,' is part of what makes us human. And to find a way to welcome the refugee and the immigrant – to be big enough and wise enough to uphold our laws and honor our values at the same time – is part of what makes us American."
Twitter, 6/20/2018

Chapter 11

Israel & Jews Quotes

Quotes On Israel and Jews (Obama)

i.   "America's commitment to Israel's security is unshakeable, and our friendship with Israel is deep and enduring."
Speech to the UN General Assembly, 9/21/2011

ii.   "To me, being pro-Israel and pro-Jewish is part and parcel with the values that I've been fighting for since I started getting involved in politics."
The Atlantic, Interview with Jeffrey Goldberg, 5/21/2015

iii.   "I care deeply about preserving that Jewish democracy, because when I think about how I came to know Israel, it was based on images of kibbutzim, and Moshe Dayan, and Golda Meir, and the sense that not only are we creating a safe Jewish homeland, but also we are remaking the world."
The Atlantic, Interview with Jeffrey Goldberg, 5/21/2015

iv.   "Precisely because I care so deeply about the State of Israel, precisely because I care so much about the Jewish people, I feel obliged to speak honestly and truthfully about what I think will be most likely to lead to long-term security, and will best position us to continue to combat anti-Semitism"
The Atlantic, Interview with Jeffrey Goldberg, 5/21/2015

v.   "Israelis and Palestinians will be better off if Palestinians reject incitement and recognize the legitimacy of Israel."
Address to the United Nations, 9/20/2016

vi.   "But Israel must recognize that it cannot permanently occupy and settle Palestinian land."
Address to the United Nations, 9/20/2016

vii.   "Bibi says that he believes in the two-state solution and yet his actions consistently have shown that if he is getting pressured to approve more settlements he will do so regardless of what he says about the importance of the two-state solution."
Interview on Israeli television, 1/10/2017

Quotes On Israel and Jews (Trump)

i. "Today we finally acknowledge the obvious: that Jerusalem is Israel's capital. This is nothing more, or less, than a recognition of reality. It is also the right thing to do. It's something that has to be done."
Statement in Diplomatic Reception Room, 12/6/2017

ii. "We want an agreement that is a great deal for the Israelis and a great deal for the Palestinians."
Statement in Diplomatic Reception Room, 12/6/2017

iii. "I ask the leaders of the region — political and religious; Israeli and Palestinian; Jewish and Christian and Muslim — to join us in the noble quest for lasting peace."
Statement in Diplomatic Reception Room, 12/6/2017

iv. "God bless Israel. God bless the Palestinians. And God bless the United States"
Statement in Diplomatic Reception Room, 12/6/2017

v. "I think Jewish people that vote for a Democrat — I think it shows either a total lack of knowledge or great disloyalty…"
Oval office meeting with Romanian president, 8/20/2019

vi. "A lot of you are in the real estate business because I know you very well. You're brutal killers, not nice people at all. But you have to vote for me, you have no choice"
Israeli-American Council Summit, 12/7/2019

vii. "(My administration) is committed to aggressively challenging and confronting anti-Semitic bigotry in every resource, and using every single weapon at our disposal."
Israeli-American Council Summit, 12/7/2019

Chapter 12

John McCain Quotes

(Quotes *about* Senator John McCain)

Quotes on John McCain (Trump)

i.   "He's not a war hero. He's a war hero because he was captured. I like people who weren't captured"
Family Leadership Summit, 7/18/15

ii.   "I always believe in apologizing if you've done something wrong, but if you read my statement, you'll see I said nothing wrong"
Interview regarding 7/18/15 statement, 7/19/2015

iii.   "So it was indeed (just proven in court papers) 'last in his class' (Annapolis) John McCain that sent the Fake Dossier to the FBI and Media hoping to have it printed BEFORE the Election."
Twitter, 3/17/2019

iv.   "I was never a fan of John McCain and never will be."
Twitter, 3/19/2019

v.   "I'm very unhappy that he didn't repeal and replace Obamacare…I think that's disgraceful. Plus, there were other things."
Remarks in Oval Office to reporters, 3/19/2019

vi.   "McCain didn't get the job done for our great vets."
Presidential Speech, Army Tank Plant, 3/20/19

vii.   "I gave him the kind of funeral that he wanted, which as president I had to approve, I don't care about this. I didn't get [a] thank you. That's OK. We sent him on the way, but I wasn't a fan of John McCain."
Presidential Speech, Army Tank Plant, 3/20/19

Quotes on John McCain (Obama)

i.   "I don't believe that Senator McCain doesn't care what's going on in the lives of Americans - I just think he doesn't know."
Acceptance speech, "The American Promise," 8/28/08

ii.   "Unlike John McCain, I will stop giving tax breaks to corporations that ship our jobs overseas, and I will start giving them to companies that create good jobs right here in America."
Acceptance speech, "The American Promise," 8/28/08

iii.   "President Bush and I are among the fortunate few who competed against John at the highest levels of politics. He made us better presidents. Just as he made the Senate better. Just as he made this country better. So, for someone like John to ask you while he was still alive to stand and speak of him when he is gone, is a precious and singular honor."
Eulogy for John McCain, 9/1/18

iv.   "John liked being unpredictable. Even a little contrarian."
Eulogy for John McCain, 9/1/18

v.   "For all of the times we sparred, I never tried to hide, and I think John came to understand, the long-standing admiration that I had for him."
Eulogy for John McCain, 9/1/18

vi.   "A warrior. A statesman. A patriot who embodied so much that is best in America."
Eulogy for John McCain, 9/1/18

Chapter 13

Media Quotes

Quotes On the Media (Trump)

i.   "I would never kill them, but I do hate them. And some of them are such lying, disgusting people."
Campaign Rally, 12/14/2015

ii. (Defending Putin) "They say, 'He killed reporters.' I said, 'Really? He says he didn't. Other people say he didn't. Who did he kill?' [They say,] 'Well, we don't know, but we hear that.' I said, 'Tell me, who did he kill!?'"
Campaign Rally, 12/14/2015

iii. "Drain the Swamp should be changed to Drain the Sewer - it's actually much worse than anyone ever thought, and it begins with the Fake News!"
Twitter, 7/24/2017

iv. "It's frankly disgusting the way the press is able to write whatever they want to write."
Comments from Oval Office, 10/11/2017

v.   "Get rid of them. (To Putin) Fake news is a great term, isn't it? You don't have this problem in Russia, but we do"
G20 Summit press conference with Putin, 6/28/2019

vi. "The Fake News hates me saying that they are the Enemy of the People only because they know it's TRUE."
Twitter, 8/5/2019

vii. "Our Primary opponent is the fake news media"
Twitter, 9/2/2019

Quotes On the Media (Obama)

i. "I swore to uphold the Constitution, and part of that Constitution is a free press…(Fox News) has a point of view that I disagree with. It's a point of view that I think is ultimately destructive for the long-term growth of a country that has a vibrant middle class and is competitive in the world.
Rolling Stone Interview, with Jann Wenner and Eric Bates, 10/14/2010

ii. "You had folks like Hearst who used their newspapers very intentionally to promote their viewpoints. I think Fox is part of that tradition – it is part of the tradition that has a very clear, undeniable point of view,"
Rolling Stone Interview, with Jann Wenner and Eric Bates, 10/14/2010

iii. "We rely on journalists to explain and describe the actions of our government. If the government controls the journalists, then it's very difficult for citizens to hold that government accountable."
Press Conference with Burmese leader, 11/14/2014

iv. "Societies that repress journalists ultimately oppress people as well, and that if you want a society that is free and vibrant and successful, part of that formula is the free flow of information, of ideas, and that requires a free press. [...] And we believe that when governments censor or control information, that ultimately undermines not only the society, but it leads to eventual encroachments on individual rights as well."
Press Conference with Burmese leader, 11/14/2014

v. "A free press helps make a nation stronger and more successful, and it makes us leaders more effective because it demands greater accountability."
Press conference in Kenya w/Kenyan president, 7/25/2015

viii.   "I have enjoyed working with all of you. That does not, of course, mean that I've enjoyed every story that you have filed. But that's the point of this relationship. You're not supposed to be sycophants, you're supposed to be skeptics. You're supposed to ask me tough questions. You're not supposed to be complimentary, but you're supposed to cast a critical eye on folks who hold enormous power and make sure that we are accountable to the people who sent us here."
Final White House Press Conference, 1/18/2017

vi.   "It shouldn't be Democratic or Republican to say that we don't threaten the freedom of the press because they say things or publish stories we don't like."
Speech at University of Illinois, 9/7/2018

Chapter 14

Race
Quotes

Quotes On Race (Obama)

i. "I am the son of a black man from Kenya and a white woman from Kansas. I was raised with the help of a white grandfather who survived a Depression to serve in Patton's Army during World War II and a white grandmother who worked on a bomber assembly line at Fort Leavenworth while he was overseas. I've gone to some of the best schools in America and lived in one of the world's poorest nations. I am married to a black American who carries within her the blood of slaves and slave owners – an inheritance we pass on to our two precious daughters. I have brothers, sisters, nieces, nephews, uncles and cousins of every race and every hue, scattered across three continents, and for as long as I live, I will never forget that in no other country on Earth is my story even possible."
"A More Perfect Union," Constitution Center, 3/18/2008

ii. "But race is an issue that I believe this nation cannot afford to ignore right now. We would be making the same mistake that Reverend Wright made in his offending sermons about America – to simplify and stereotype and amplify the negative to the point that it distorts reality."
"A More Perfect Union," Constitution Center, 3/18/2008

iii. "Legalized discrimination – where blacks were prevented, often through violence, from owning property, or loans were not granted to African-American business owners, or black homeowners could not access FHA mortgages, or blacks were excluded from unions or the police force or the fire department – meant that black families could not amass any meaningful wealth to bequeath to future generations."
"A More Perfect Union," Constitution Center, 3/18/2008

iv.   "That's an interesting question. Thank you.
I believe that under the surface all people are the same. Now part of that
is my own heritage and my own background. My father was a black
man from Africa. My mother was a white woman in the United States,
whose ancestors had come from England and Scotland. My mother
remarried, and then we moved to Indonesia. So I have a half-sister who
is Asian. I have nieces who are half Chinese. And so in my own family,
I've got the genetic strains of everybody. And it gives me confidence --
confidence that's been reinforced as President -- that people are all
essentially the same. Similar hopes, similar dreams, similar strengths,
similar weaknesses. But we're also all bound by history and culture and
habits. And so conflicts arise, in part, because of some weaknesses in
human nature. When we feel threatened, then we like to strike out
against people who are not like us. When change is happening too
quickly, and we try to hang on to those things that we think could give
us a solid foundation. And sometimes the organizing principles are
around issues like race, or religion. When there are times of scarcity,
then people can turn on each other."
Young Leaders of the Americas Town Hall, Buenos Aires, Argentina, 3/23/2016

v.   "With an open heart, we can abandon the overheated rhetoric and the
oversimplification that reduces whole categories of our fellow
Americans not just to opponents, but to enemies."
Memorial for Fallen Dallas Police Officers, 7/12/16

vi.   "With an open heart, we can worry less about which side has been
wronged, and worry more about joining sides to do right. Because the
vicious killer of these police officers, they won't be the last person who
tries to make us turn on one other."
Memorial for Fallen Dallas Police Officers, 7/12/16

vii.   "It's important for us to also understand that the phrase 'Black Lives
Matter' simply refers to the notion that there's a specific vulnerability for
African Americans that needs to be addressed. It's not meant to suggest
that other lives don't matter. It's to suggest that other folks aren't
experiencing this particular vulnerability."
ABC Town Hall, 7/14/2016

Quotes On Race (Trump)

i.   "We have never discriminated and we never would"
Statement to NY Times, (in response to Department of Justice receiving multiple allegations that the Trump organization discriminated against blacks), October 1973

ii.   "A well-educated black has a tremendous advantage over a well-educated white in terms of the job market…I've said on one occasion, even about myself, if I were starting off today, I would love to be a well-educated black, because I believe they do have an actual advantage."
Interview with Bryant Gumbel, 1989

iii.   "Well, you've got David Duke just joined — a big racist, a problem. I mean, this is not exactly the people you want in your party"
The Today Show, 2/14/2000

iv.   "I've always had a great relationship with the blacks"
NY Talk Radio, 4/14/2011

v.   "Well, just so you understand, I don't know anything about David Duke. OK? I don't know anything about what you're even talking about with white supremacy or white supremacists. So, I don't know. I don't know, did he endorse me or what's going on, because, you know, I know nothing about David Duke. I know nothing about white supremacists. And so you're asking me a question that I'm supposed to be talking about people that I know nothing about. You wouldn't want me to condemn a group that I know nothing about. I would have to look. If you would send me a list of the groups, I will do research on them. And, certainly, I would disavow if I thought there was something wrong.
CNN interview with Jake Tapper, 2/28/2016

vi.   "Hillary Clinton is a bigot who sees people of color only as votes, not as human beings worthy of a better future,"
Prepared remarks, Mississippi speech, 8/24/2016

vii.   "I am the least racist person there is anywhere in the world"
       Statement on White House Lawn, 7/30/2019

viii. "These sinister ideologies must be defeated. Hate has no place in
       America."
       *Speech after the El Paso hate crime shooting which killed 22 Hispanic people,
       8/5/19*

Chapter 15

Socialism
Quotes

Quotes On Socialism (Trump)

i. "Here, in the United States, we are alarmed by new calls to adopt socialism in our country."
State of the Union Address, 2/5/2019

ii. "We know that socialism is not about justice, it's not about equality, it's not about lifting up the poor. Socialism is about one thing only: power for the ruling class."
Remarks to Venezuelan-American Community, 2/18/19

iii. "Socialism is a sad and discredited ideology rooted in the total ignorance of history and human nature."
Remarks to Venezuelan-American Community, 2/18/19

iv. "Socialism, eventually, must always give rise to tyranny, which it does."
Remarks to Venezuelan-American Community, 2/18/19

v. "They want to run healthcare, run transportation and finance, run energy, education, run everything."
Remarks to Venezuelan-American Community, 2/18/19

vi. "There is nothing less democratic than socialism"
Remarks to Venezuelan-American Community, 2/18/19

Quotes On Socialism (Obama)

i. "You should be practical, and just choose from what works. You don't have to worry about whether it neatly fits into socialist theory or capitalist theory. You should just decide what works."
Young Leaders of the Americas Town Hall, Buenos Aires, Argentina, 3/23/2016

ii. "The market system produces a lot of wealth and goods and services and innovation and it also gives individuals freedom because they have initiative."
Young Leaders of the Americas Town Hall, Buenos Aires, Argentina, 3/23/2016

iii. "What you'll find is the most successful societies and economies are the ones that are rooted in a market-based system but also realize a market does not work by itself. It has to have a social and moral and ethical and community basis."
Young Leaders of the Americas Town Hall, Buenos Aires, Argentina, 3/23/2016

iv. "Every child in Cuba gets a basic education. Medical care, the life expectancy of Cubans is equivalent to the United States despite it being a very poor country because they have access to health care. That's a huge achievement. They should be congratulated. But, you drive around Havana and you see this economy is not working. It looks like it did in the 1950s"
Young Leaders of the Americas Town Hall, Buenos Aires, Argentina, 3/23/2016

v. "There's only so much you can eat. There's only so big a house you can have."
Speech in South Africa, 7/18/2018

vi. "The average American doesn't think we have to completely tear down the system and remake it."□
Speech to Democratic donors, 11/16/2019

Chapter 16

Terrorism
Quotes

Quotes On Terrorism (Obama)

i. "Good evening. Tonight I can report to the American people and to the world that the United States has conducted an operation that killed Osama bin Laden, top leader of al-Qaeda.
Special Address to the Nation, 5/1/2011

ii. "Groups like ISIL and al-Qaida want to make this war a war between Islam and America, or between Islam and the West."
Press conference, 6/14/2016

iii. "They want to claim that they are the true leaders of over a billion Muslims around the world who reject their crazy notions. They want us to validate them, by implying that they speak for those billion-plus people, that they speak for Islam. That's their propaganda. That's how they recruit."
Press conference, 6/14/2016

iv. "And if we fall into the trap of painting all Muslims with a broad brush, and imply that we are at war with an entire religion, then we are doing the terrorists' work for them."
Press conference, 6/14/2016

v. "It makes Muslim Americans feel like their government is betraying them. It betrays the very values America stands for. We've gone through moments in our history before when we acted out of fear, and we came to regret it…This is a country founded on basic freedoms — including freedom of religion."
Press conference, 6/14/2016

vi. "So, someone seriously thinks that we don't know who we're fighting? If there's anyone out there who thinks we're confused about who our enemies are, that would come as a surprise to the thousands of terrorists who ... we've taken off the battlefield."
Press conference, 6/14/2016

vii.   "What exactly would using this label accomplish? What exactly would it
change? Would it make ISIS less committed to trying to kill Americans?
Would it bring in more allies? Is there a military strategy that is served
by this? The answer is none of the above. Calling a threat by a different
name does not make it go away. This is a political distraction."
Press conference, 6/14/2016

Quotes On Terrorism (Trump)

i.   "In the 20th Century, the United States defeated Fascism, Nazism, and Communism. Now, a different threat challenges our world: Radical Islamic Terrorism"
How To Make America Safe Again speech, 8/15/2016

ii. "Just like we couldn't defeat communism without acknowledging that communism exists – or explaining its evils – we can't defeat Radical Islamic Terrorism unless we do the same."
How To Make America Safe Again speech, 8/15/2016

iii. "Anyone who cannot name our enemy, is not fit to lead this country. Anyone who cannot condemn the hatred, oppression and violence of Radical Islam lacks the moral clarity to serve as our President."
How To Make America Safe Again speech, 8/15/2016

iv. "Holy sites desecrated. Christians driven from their homes and hunted for extermination. ISIS rounding-up what it calls the "nation of the cross" in a campaign of genocide. We cannot let this evil continue."
How To Make America Safe Again speech, 8/15/2016

v.   "With one episode of bad judgment after another, Hillary Clinton's policies launched ISIS onto the world.
Yet, as she threw the Middle East into violent turmoil, things turned out well for her. The Clintons made almost $60 million in gross income while she was Secretary of State."
How To Make America Safe Again speech, 8/15/2016

vi. "We will reinforce old alliances and form new ones – and unite the civilized world against Radical Islamic Terrorism, which we will eradicate completely from the face of the Earth."
Inaugural Address, 1/20/2017

vii.   "Here at this summit we will discuss many interests we share together.
        But above all we must be united in pursuing the one goal that transcends
        every other consideration. That goal is to meet history's great test—to
        conquer extremism and vanquish the forces of terrorism. Young Muslim
        boys and girls should be able to grow up free from fear, safe from
        violence, and innocent of hatred. And young Muslim men and women
        should have the chance to build a new era of prosperity for themselves
        and their peoples. With God's help, this summit will mark the beginning
        of the end for those who practice terror and spread its vile creed."
        Arab Islamic American Summit Speech, 5/21/2017

viii.   "Last night, the United States brought the world's number one terrorist
        leader to justice. Abu Bakr al-Baghdadi is dead. He was the founder
        and leader of ISIS, the most ruthless and violent terror organization
        anywhere in the world."
        Special Address to the nation 10/27/2019

Chapter 17

Vladimir Putin/ Russia Quotes

(Quotes *about* Putin and Russia)

Quotes On Putin & Russia (Trump)

i. "I do have a relationship, and I can tell you that he's very interested in what we're doing here today"
MSNBC Moscow interview (re: Miss Universe Pageant), 11/9/2013

ii. "You know, I was in Moscow a couple months ago, I own the Miss Universe pageant and they treated me so great…Putin even sent me a present, beautiful present, with a beautiful note, I spoke to all of his people. You look at what he's doing with President Obama he's like toying with him. He's toying with him."
CPAC Conference, 3/6/2014

iii. "Putin has become a big hero in Russia with an all time high popularity. Obama, on the other hand, has fallen to his lowest ever numbers. SAD."
Twitter, 3/21/2014

iv. "Putin has an 80 percent popularity in this country where I thought they didn't even like him a year ago. But he's so outsmarting the United States, and all of a sudden the people in Russia like him."
National Press Club Interview, transcript, p8, 5/27/2014

v. "I was in Russia, I was in Moscow recently, and I spoke indirectly and directly with President Putin, who could not have been nicer."
National Press Club Interview, transcript p16, 5/27/2014

vi. "But, as far as the Ukraine is concerned, and you could Syria—as far as Syria, I like—if Putin wants to go in, and I got to know him very well because we were both on 60 Minutes, we were stablemates, and we did very well that night. But, you know that. But, if Putin wants to go and knocked the hell out of ISIS, I am all for it, 100 percent, and I can't understand how anybody would be against it…"
Fox Business Debate 11/10/2015

vii. "It is always a great honor to be so nicely complimented by a man so highly respected within his own country and beyond."
ABC News. In response to Putin's remarks, 12/17/2015

viii.   "I have no relationship with Putin… I have no relationship with
        Putin…I've never met him...I don't think I've ever met him… I never
        met him…I've never spoken with him on the phone"
        ABC News interview with George Stephanopoulos, 7/31/2016

ix.   "The people of Crimea, from what I've heard, would rather be with
        Russia than where they were."
        ABC News interview with George Stephanopoulos, 7/31/2016

x.   "Russia, if you're listening, I hope you're able to find the 30,000 emails
        that are missing."
        Press Conference, 7/27/2016

Quotes On Putin & Russia (Obama)

i. "Mr. Putin had to go into Syria not out of strength, but out of weakness because his client Mr. Assad was crumbling and it was insufficient for him to send arms and money."
White House news conference, 10/2/2015

ii. "In a world that left the age of empire behind, we see Russia attempting to recover lost glory through force"
Address to the United Nations, 9/20/2016

iii. "If Russia continues to interfere in the affairs of its neighbors, it may be popular at home, it may fuel nationalist fervor for a time, but over time it's also going to diminish its stature and make its borders less secure."
Address to the United Nations, 9/20/2016

iv. "History shows that strongmen are left with two paths — permanent crackdown, which sparks strife at home; or scapegoating enemies abroad, which can lead to war."
Address to the United Nations, 9/20/2016

v. "Not much happens in Russia without Vladimir Putin…This is pretty hierarchical operation. Last I checked, there's not a lot of debate and democratic deliberation, particularly when it comes to policies directed at the United States."
White House Press Conference, 12/16/2016

vi. "There was a survey some of you saw, now this is just one poll, but a pretty credible source, 37% of Republican voters approve of Putin," Obama said. "Over a third of Republican voters approve of Vladimir Putin, the former head of the KGB. Ronald Reagan would roll over in his grave."
White House Press Conference, 12/16/2016

vii. "Because of the fierceness of the partisan battle, you've started to see certain folks in the Republican Party and Republican voters suddenly finding a government and individuals who stand contrary to everything we stand for as being OK because that's how much we dislike Democrats."
White House Press Conference, 12/16/2016

viii. "I mean, think about it, some of the people who historically have been very critical of me for engaging with Russians and having conversations with them also endorsed the president-elect even as he was saying that we should stop sanctioning Russia and being tough on them…"
White House Press Conference, 12/16/2016

ix. "He was very complimentary of Mr. Putin personally. That wasn't news. The president-elect during the campaign said so. And some folks who had made a career out of being anti-Russian didn't say anything about it."
White House Press Conference, 12/16/2016

x. "And then after the election, suddenly they're asking, 'Why didn't you tell us that maybe the Russians were trying to help our candidate?' Well, come on."
White House Press Conference, 12/16/2016

Chapter 18

Quotes On Their Opposing Party

Quotes On their Opposing Party (Obama)

i.   "The accepted wisdom that drives many advocacy groups and Democratic activists these days goes like this: The Republican Party has been able to consistently win elections not by expanding its base but by vilifying Democrats, driving wedges into the electorate, energizing its right wing, and disciplining those who stray from the party line. If the Democrats ever want to get back into power, then they will have to take up the same approach."
The Audacity of Hope, 2006

ii.   "We lose elections and hope for the courts to foil Republican plans. We lost the courts and wait for a White House scandal. And increasingly we feel the need to match the Republican right in stridency and hardball tactics."
The Audacity of Hope, 2006

iii.   "For it's precisely the pursuit of ideological purity, the rigid orthodoxy and the sheer predictability of our current political debate, that keeps us from finding new ways to meet the challenges we face as a country. It's what keeps us locked in "either/or" thinking: the notion that we can have only big government or no government; the assumption that we must either tolerate forty-six million without health insurance or embrace 'socialized medicine.' It is such doctrinaire thinking and stark partisanship that have turned Americans off of politics."
The Audacity of Hope, 2006

iv.   "It's a bill that's paid for, a bill that won't add to the deficit. It has been written by Democrats and Republicans. It's a bill that's been praised by the Chamber of Commerce. And yet a minority of Republican senators have been using legislative tactics to prevent the bill from even getting to a vote."
Press conference, 9/10/2010

v.   "The policies that we have put in place have moved us in the right direction, and the policies that the Republicans are offering right now are the exact policies that got us into this mess."
Press conference, 9/10/2010

vi. "As I said, this was written by Democrats and Republicans. This is a
bill that traditionally you'd probably get 90 percent or 100 percent
Republican support. But we've been playing politics for the last several
months. And if the Republican leadership is prepared to get serious
about doing something for families that are hurting out there, I would
love to talk to them."
Press conference, 9/10/2010

vii. "And what I've got is the Republicans holding middle-class tax relief
hostage because they're insisting we've got to give tax relief to
millionaires and billionaires to the tune of about $100,000 per
millionaire, which would cost over the course of 10 years, $700 billion,
and that economists say is probably the worst way to stimulate the
economy."
Press conference, 9/10/2010

viii. "I do feel a responsibility as president of the United States to speak out
with respect to areas where I think the Republican party's wrong, but to
pledge to work with them on those things that I think will advance the
causes of security and prosperity and justice and inclusiveness in
America."
Press conference with Greek Prime Minister, 11/15/2016

ix. "The Tea Party I have huge disagreements with, obviously. But I give
them credit for having activated themselves. And they made a difference
in terms of moving the Republican Party, in terms of moving the country
in a particular direction. It's a direction I disagreed with. But it showed
that, in fact, you get involved, if your voice is heard it has an impact."
60 Minutes interview with Steve Croft, 1/15/2017

Quotes On their Opposing Party (Trump)

i. "Happy New Year to all, including to my many enemies and those who have fought me and lost so badly they just don't know what to do. Love"
Twitter, 12/31/2016

ii. "You've got half the room going totally crazy, wild, they loved everything, they wanna do something great for our country, and you have the other side, even on positive news, really positive news, like that, they were like death, and un-American, un-American. Somebody said treasonous, I mean, yeah I guess, why not? Can we call that treason, why not?"
Speech in Ohio, 2/4/2018

iii. "Now all of a sudden they're big open border people. It's a whole big con job. In the meantime, people are suffering because of the Democrats. So we've created, and they've created, and they've let it happen — a massive child-smuggling industry."
Oval Office Statement, 6/21/2018

iv. "The only reason to vote for a Democrat is if you are tired of winning."
Twitter, 10/2/2018

v. "If they wanted me to, but I think we'll probably pass."
Answering reporter's question on South Lawn as to whether he would call President Obama and President Clinton after fake pipe bombs were sent to them by mail. 10/26/2018

vi. "Tone down, no. Could tone up. I think I've been toned down, if you want to know the truth."
Answering reporter's question on South Lawn as to whether he might tone down the rhetoric in light of the fake mail bombs recently sent to the previous two Democrat presidents. 10/26/2018

vii.   "The crime was by the Democrats. The crime was by the Democrats. There is no legal basis for impeachment. It's a big witch hunt. Everybody knows it, including the Democrats."
Remarks to reporters on the White House Lawn, 6/2/2019

viii.   "The leading voices of the Democrat Party are left-wing extremists who reject everything our nation stands for"
Rally speech, (North Carolina), 7/17/19

ix.   "The Democrats have become too extreme. And they've become, frankly, too dangerous to govern. They've gone wacko"
Rally speech, (Iowa), 10/10/2019

Chapter 19

Quotes On Their Own Party

Quotes On Their Own Party (Trump)

    i.   (On Rand Paul) "Truly weird Senator Rand Paul of Kentucky reminds me of a spoiled brat without a properly functioning brain. He was terrible at DEBATE!"
Twitter, 8/10/2015

    ii.   (On Jeb Bush) "Jeb is an embarrassment to himself and his family, and the Republican Party has essentially-- they're not even listening to Jeb"
Meet The Press, 12/20/2015

    iii.   (On Marco Rubio) "Little Marco Rubio, the lightweight no show Senator from Florida, is set to be the "puppet" of the special interest Koch brothers. WATCH!"
Twitter, 2/28/2016

    iv.   (On John Kasich and Ted Cruz) "Wow, just announced that Lyin' Ted and Kasich are going to collude in order to keep me from getting the Republican nomination. DESPERATION!"
Twitter, 4/24/2016

    v.   (On John Kasich) "Did you see him? He has a news conference, all the time when he's eating. I have never seen a human being eat in such a disgusting fashion"
Rally (Rhode Island), 4/25/2016

    vi.   (On Ted Cruz) "He's not Lyin' Ted anymore. He's Beautiful Ted"
Comments on South Lawn a few weeks prior to Sen. Cruz's re-election, 10/22/2018

    vii.   "The Republicans have to get tougher and fight… we have some that are great fighters, but they have to get tougher and fight, because the Democrats are trying to hurt the Republican party before the election."
White House Cabinet Meeting, 10/21/2019

    viii.   "The Never Trumper Republicans, though on respirators with not many left, are in certain ways worse and more dangerous for our Country than the Do Nothing Democrats. Watch out for them, they are human scum!"
Twitter, 10/23/2019

Quotes On their Own Party (Obama)

i. "When we are divided and our politics is focused on dividing, then I think we're less successful, not just from the perspective of the Democratic Party or the Republican Party but from the perspective of the nation as a whole."
Meet The Press, with Tim Russert, 11/7/2004

ii. "I didn't take Sen. Biden's comments personally, but obviously they were historically inaccurate… African-American presidential candidates like Jesse Jackson, Shirley Chisholm, Carol Moseley Braun and Al Sharpton gave a voice to many important issues through their campaigns, and no one would call them inarticulate."
Responding to his Democratic primary opponent's comment that Obama was the first "mainstream" black presidential candidate and that he was "clean" and "articulate" 1/31/07

iii. "You're likeable enough, Hillary"
Democratic primary debate against Hillary Clinton, 1/5/2008

iv. (On Bill Clinton) "The former president, who I think all of us have a lot of regard for, has taken his advocacy on behalf of his wife to a level that I think is pretty troubling. He continues to make statements that are not supported by the facts"
Democratic primary debate against Hillary Clinton, 1/21/2008

v. "I think that the Democratic Party is a big tent, which means that there are positions I may not agree with… what I want to try to do is unify the two wings of the Democratic Party- what's considered the more progressive wing of the Democratic Party and the more centrist wing of the party. I think we can craft an approach that is more American, pro-worker, pro-business, pro-growth."
Interview with David Mark of Politico.com, 2/11/2008

vi. "The politics around trade has always been tough, particularly in the Democratic party, because people have memories of outsourcing and job loss."
Press Conference with Italian Prime Minister, 4/17/2015

vii.   "I think it's a healthy thing for the Democratic Party to go through some
        reflection."
        Press conference, 11/14/2016

viii.   "I invigorated the grassroots in the Republican Party as well as the
        Democratic Party."
        ABC News interview with George Stephanopoulos, 1/8/2017

Chapter 20

Quotes About
Each Other

Obama On Trump

i.   "Look, the people have spoken. Donald Trump will be the next president, the 45th president of the United States. And it will be up to him to set up a team that he thinks will serve him well and reflect his policies. And those who didn't vote for him have to recognize that that's how democracy works. That's how this system operates,"
Press conference, 11/14/2016

ii.   "He was able to tap into, yes the anxieties, but also the enthusiasm of his voters in a way that was impressive"
Press conference, 11/14/2016

iii.   "I don't think he is ideological. I think ultimately he is pragmatic …and that can serve him well."
Press conference, 11/14/2016

iv.   "There are going to be certain elements of his temperament that will not serve him well unless he recognizes them and corrects them…When you're a candidate and you say something that is inaccurate or controversial, it has less impact than it does when you're President of the United States. Everybody around the world is paying attention. Markets move. National security issues require a level of precision in order to make sure that you don't make mistakes.
I think he recognizes that this is different, and so do the American people."
Press conference, 11/14/2016

v.   "Gestures matter, and how he reaches out to groups that may not have supported him, how he signals his interest in their issues or concerns, I think those are the kinds of things that can set a tone that will help move things forward once he has actually taken office."
Press conference, 11/14/2016

vi.   "He's just capitalizing on resentments that politicians have been fanning for years... Appealing to tribe, appealing to fear, pitting one group against another, telling people that order and security will be restored if it weren't for those who don't look like us or don't sound like us or don't pray like we do, that's an old playbook. It's as old as time. And in a healthy democracy it doesn't work."
Speech, University of Illinois, 9/7/2018

vii.   "Demagogues promise simple fixes to complex problems. They promise to fight for the little guy even as they cater to the wealthiest and the most powerful. They promise to clean up corruption and then plunder away. They start undermining norms that ensure accountability, try to change the rules to entrench their power further. And they appeal to racial nationalism that's barely veiled, if veiled at all."
Speech, University of Illinois, 9/7/2018

viii. "It's not conservative. It sure isn't normal. It's radical. It's a vision that says the protection of our power and those who back us is all that matters"
Speech, University of Illinois, 9/7/2018

ix.   "We're supposed to stand up to discrimination. And we're sure as heck supposed to stand up, clearly and unequivocally, to Nazi sympathizers. How hard can that be? Saying that Nazis are bad."
Speech, University of Illinois, 9/7/2018

Trump On Obama

i.   "Growing up no one knew him."
Good Morning America interview, 3/17/2011

ii.   "Today I am very proud of myself because I was able to accomplish something that nobody else has been able to accomplish. I was just informed that our president has finally released a birth certificate. I want to look at it. But I hope it's true…I am really honored in having played such a big role in hopefully…getting rid of this issue"
Press Conference, NH, 4/27/2011

iii.   "Look, I made the keynote speech in North Carolina this weekend. The biggest applause was when the issue of birthplace was brought up."
CNBC interview, 6/5/2012

iv.   "Many people will be surprised at what is about to be released concerning Barack Obama's background. I, for one, won't be."
Twitter, 8/22/2012

v.   "An extremely credible source has called my office and told me that Barack Obama's birth certificate is a fraud."
Twitter, 9/6/2012

vi.   "Well, I don't know, was there a birth certificate? You tell me. You know some people say that was not his birth certificate. I'm saying, I don't know. Nobody does."
ABC interview, Jon Karl, 8/11/2013

vii.   "So look, there are three things that could happen, and one of them did happen. He was perhaps born in Kenya, very simple, okay? He was perhaps born in this country, but said he was born in Kenya. Because if you say you were born in Kenya, you got aid, and you got into colleges. And people were doing that."
National Press Club Interview, transcript, 5/27/2014

viii.   "If I decide to run for office, I'll produce my tax returns. Absolutely. I
        would love to do that…He should have come clean over the years. If
        you remember the very famous story where I offered him $5 million if
        he showed some basic records and he never took me up on it and that
        would be for charity."
        Ireland AM TV3, interview with Colette Fitzpatrick 5/20/2014

ix.   "I offered $5 million just to see some basic records…Just some basic
        things on applications to colleges. I'd love to see what's put down. Why
        didn't a man take $5 million for his favorite charity?"
        National Press Club Interview, transcript, 5/27/2014

x.   "He is the founder of ISIS"
        Multiple rallies, August, 2016

xi.   "Putin's been a leader, far more than Obama has been."
        NBC's Commander In Chief Forum, 9/7/2016

xii.   "President Barack Obama was born in the United States, period. Now
        we all want to get back to making America strong and great again.
        Thank you."
        Statement from Trump Hotel, DC, 9/16/2016

xiii.   "I don't know why he wouldn't release his records. I was the one who got
        him to release his birth certificate and I think I did a good job"
        Presidential Debate, 9/26/2016

xiv.   "How low has President Obama gone to tap my phones during the very
        sacred election process? This is Nixon/Watergate. Bad (or sick) guy!"
        Twitter, 3/4/2017

xv.   "I've gone to numerous G-7 meetings, and I guess … because Putin
        outsmarted him, President Obama thought it wasn't a good thing to have
        Russia in."
        G7 Press Conference, Biarritz, France, 8/26/2019

xvi.   "President Putin totally outsmarted President Obama on Crimea and
        other things including the 'red line' in the sand."
        Remarks on White House Lawn, 8/28/2019

Quotes On Their Own Legacy

President Trump On His Own Legacy

"Nobody has ever done so much in the first two years of a presidency as this administration. Nobody. Nobody…And at my direction, the Pentagon is now working to create the sixth branch of the American armed forces. It's called the Space Force. Very important. Very, very important. I withdrew the United States from the horrible, one-sided Iran nuclear deal, which was a disaster. And we have recognized the capital of Israel and opened the American embassy in Jerusalem."
Political Rally, Biloxi, Mississippi, 11/26/2018

"I accomplished the military. I accomplished the tax cuts. I accomplished the regulation cuts. I accomplished so much. The economy is the number-one economy in the world."
Remarks at signing Executive Order, the White House, 1/31/2019

President Obama On His Own Legacy

"It's one of the few regrets of my presidency that the rancor and suspicion between the parties has gotten worse instead of better."
State of the Union Address 1/12/2016

"We have helped, I think, shape a generation to think about being inclusive, being fair, caring about the environment. And they will have growing influence year by year, which means that America over time will continue to get better."
Rolling Stone interview by Jann Wenner, 11/9/16

About the Author:

Lincoln Roberts, M.Ed, is an educator with a passion for US History and US Presidents. He lives in New Jersey.

Thank you and Acknowledgements

The author wishes to thank Presidents Obama and Trump for providing insight into their thinking through their own words.

www.ingramcontent.com/pod-product-compliance
Lightning Source LLC
Chambersburg PA
CBHW051216250726
48655CB00006B/2434